PAKISTAN AND THE WORLD BANK
PARTNERS IN PROGRESS

THE WORLD BANK
Washington, D.C.

The views and interpretations in this booklet are not necessarily those of the Executive Directors of the World Bank or the countries they represent. The map appearing as frontispiece was prepared exclusively for the convenience of readers of this booklet; the denominations used and the boundaries shown do not imply, on the part of the World Bank and its affiliates, any judgment on the legal status of any territory or any endorsement or acceptance of such boundaries.

Photograph Credits

Cover: B. Martin-Roland
Page 3:   Courtesy Embassy of Pakistan, Washington
Page 10:   John M. Courtney
Page 19:   Tomas Sennett
Page 27:   B. Martin-Roland
Page 36:   B. Martin-Roland
Page 47:   B. Martin-Roland
Page 59:   Tomas Sennett
Page 71:   B. Martin-Roland

Cover

Students at the government primary school for boys at Kala Gujran, Jhelum District, Punjab Province, Pakistan. The school was built with World Bank assistance. The development of human resources through education has become a principal focus both of Pakistan's current development plan and of World Bank lending to the country.

The design used on the title page and on each chapter opening page is from an architectural motif on the Sheesh Mahal, which was built inside Lahore Fort by Mogul emperor Shāh Jāhan.

Pakistan and the World Bank was written under the auspices of the Public Affairs Division, Information and Public Affairs Department, The World Bank.

ISBN 0-8213-0723-1

Contents

INTRODUCTION

THROUGH MID-1983, Pakistan's economy experienced rapid growth. Real growth of overall national output and of specific components such as agriculture, industry, and exports has been at rates which are very respectable compared with the performance of most developing countries during the same period. Although still facing serious strains, the current account deficit and budgetary gap have been considerably reduced in relation to gross domestic product (GDP) despite a sharp deterioration in terms of trade, a decline in net aid flows in real terms, and falling remittances from Pakistanis working abroad.

Much of the credit for this improved performance should go to changes in government policies designed to make better use of financial and physical resources available to the country. One important outcome is the encouragement now given to the private sector to participate more fully in the expansion and diversification of the economy. The country is fortunate in having a large entrepreneurial class, which has responded vigorously to the opportunities now being made available to it.

This booklet discusses the changes that Pakistan has witnessed during its current phase of strong growth (more than 6 percent a year since 1977). Pakistan's effort to create an environment favorable to the efficient allocation and use of resources is particularly noted. In a country that has approximately 90 million people and many historical handicaps, change can be only gradual. As the booklet points out, much remains to be done to ensure that rapid growth is sustained and that its benefits reach the entire population. Nevertheless, the progress that Pakistan has made in restructuring its economy in the past twenty years—highlighted by the fall in the share of agriculture in GDP from 40 to 27 percent—encourages confidence in its ability to cope with the tasks that lie ahead.

Like any other developing country, Pakistan is critically dependent on the flow of external resources to augment national savings. A significant part of this flow has come from the World Bank, largely in the form of highly concessional credits from the International Development Association (IDA) but with loans from the International Bank for Reconstruction and Development (IBRD) increasing as IDA resources become limited.[1] This assistance has been offered in the context of a policy dialogue to help the Government of Pakistan develop and refine its policy options, particularly in relation to the principal sectors—energy, industry, and agriculture—which have a large bearing on the economy's future. The dialogue has been supported in important instances by studies (financed by technical assistance credits) to pinpoint and formulate programs of reform.

By mid-1985, both the IBRD and IDA had made cumulative commitments of $3.2 billion (all dollars are U.S. dollars; billion is one thousand million) to Pakistan. This amount includes the Bank's share of involvement with other funding agencies in a major program to develop the water resources of the Indus Basin during a twenty-year period. The Bank's commitments were divided thus: approximately 30 percent

1. The expressions "the World Bank" and "the Bank" as used in this booklet mean both the International Bank for Reconstruction and Development and the International Development Association. The IBRD has a second affiliate, the International Finance Corporation. The Bank has one central purpose: to help raise standards of living in developing countries by channeling financial resources from developed countries to the developing world.

Islamabad, the capital of Pakistan, is a new city. Its construction began in 1960, and by the early 1980s it had about 200,000 people.

for agriculture and irrigation; 28 percent for industry, including funds for imports of essential inputs; 18 percent for transport, telecommunications, and public utility services; 14 percent for energy, including power, gas pipelines, and petroleum; 5 percent for social programs, including education, population, and urban development; and 5 percent for structural adjustment and technical assistance. In addition to the contribution that the World Bank itself makes, it also plays a part in mobilizing resources from other donors and the market by fostering greater understanding of Pakistan's needs. Annual meetings of the Pakistan Consortium (a consortium of bilateral and multilateral lending agencies) chaired by the Bank are an important part of this endeavor.

This booklet starts with a review of the broad issues facing Pakistan and how these are being addressed through a program of structural adjustments in the economy. Subsequent sections focus on the main facets of the economy—agriculture, irrigation, power, oil and gas, industry, and human resources—to show what Pakistan has achieved and what remains to be done to consolidate the gains and to carry them forward. The treatment of issues is necessarily selective and brief because of the limitations in space of a booklet intended to serve as an introduction to a dynamic economy in which there is increasing international interest.

PAKISTAN'S ECONOMY
Agendas for Reform

WITH A GROWTH RATE of more than 6 percent since 1977, Pakistan's economy has made a remarkable turnaround after a slowdown that persisted for much of the 1970s. The country's performance owes a great deal to reforms in economic policies carried out since the present government came to office in 1977. Pakistan is now getting more out of its existing assets and is making fairly prudent use of available resources to create new ones according to a well-conceived scheme of priorities. A particular effort has been made to provide an environment in which private enterprise can make a fuller contribution to the country's growth.

Although considerable headway has been made since Pakistan resumed medium-term planning by launching its fifth five-year plan (1979–84), a great deal remains to be done to lay the foundations of sustained growth. Since population will continue to increase by 2.5 to 3.0 percent a year for the foreseeable future, Pakistan cannot afford a slackening of growth if it is to ensure minimum acceptable improvements in the welfare of a population already above the 90 million mark. The two main weaknesses of its economy are a low level of national savings and a persistently large current account deficit. Unless both are urgently tackled, growth will be increasingly constrained by the inadequacy of external resources—more so because of the discouraging outlook for any significant increase in concessional aid in real terms. The vulnerability of Pakistan in this regard is evident from the facts that exports pay for only 45 percent of imports in a typical year and that over a quarter of domestic investments in the fifth plan period were financed by foreign savings. Despite these external inputs, fixed investments in the economy were at the low level of 13.6 percent of gross national product (GNP) in 1982–83. As a result, the renewal and replacement of capital stock are seriously in arrears.

A Series of Reforms

The government recognizes the economic challenge it faces and has embarked on a series of reforms to tackle the major weaknesses in the country's economic structure. As a first installment, in mid-1982 it started a program of structural adjustment to address in an integrated manner the problems the country was facing in several important sectors (agriculture and irrigation, energy, and industry) and in development planning. This effort was underpinned by a structural adjustment lending operation (SAL) that consisted of a $60 million IBRD loan and an $80 million IDA credit. This SAL program included a number of significant reforms in policies and programs in agriculture and irrigation, energy, and industry and in government development planning.

In agriculture and irrigation, the change involved reorienting investment toward faster-yielding projects with the aim of getting quick increases in output and income from sales to domestic and foreign markets. The focus was on rehabilitating the irrigation system, one of the largest in the world, to improve the efficiency with which scarce water was utilized at the farm level. Simultaneous action was taken to increase the availability of the matching inputs needed to translate better water supply into higher crop output. To encourage farmers to put their best foot forward, the government made sure that decisions on input and output prices were made in a coordinated and timely manner before each cropping season. The Agricultural Prices Commission was given a large role in formulating price policies in the overall context of the government's commitment to align domestic input and output prices in a carefully phased manner with those obtaining in the international marketplace.

In energy, shortages of power and gas underlined the need for a larger and better-coordinated investment effort to reduce the need for imported energy. It was decided to draw as much as possible on the domestic and foreign private sector both to augment the resources the government could itself deploy and to harness technical and managerial expertise. Recognizing that pricing policies which discouraged investors were a factor inhibiting development of the country's considerable gas resources, the government undertook a series of changes in the prices payable to producers. At the consumer level, the price of oil was already in line with the level in the international market while that of gas was to be brought closer to parity through successive increases in domestic prices. In addition, the government redefined its own role in oil and gas exploration and development, as is evident from the offer of leases to private companies for areas formerly earmarked for a state-owned corporation.

In industry, there was a clear need for increased investments for two pressing reasons. One was to generate export surpluses and save on imports which could be efficiently produced at home. The other was to continue the ongoing changes in the structure of the economy to maintain the momentum of growth. The government decided that new investments in industry should come primarily from the private sector; this would provide an incentive to generate savings and deploy them productively. To create an environment conducive to private initiatives, the government outlined a new policy framework offering safeguards against nationalization and restricting public investment in industry to consolidation and completion of existing enterprises. There were to be no new industrial starts in the public sector except as a last resort. In such a contingency, the government said it would prefer joint ventures with the private sector. In principle, this left the entire industrial field wide open to the private sector. Public enterprises, which play an important role in several principal industries, were to operate increasingly on commercial lines. For a start, performance criteria (underpinned by a system of management bonuses) were laid down for virtually all public manufacturing enterprises.

In development planning, the limited resources available to the government were redirected from public investment in manufacturing and subsidies for fertilizers to high-priority investments in agriculture and irrigation, energy, and the social sectors. At the same time, it was decided to improve project preparation, implementation, and monitoring to ensure the efficient and timely use of resources. There was also a concern that delays in the execution of plan projects, along with those caused by lags in finding domestic resources, were undermining the coherence of the plan and its strategy.

Among the steps taken to strengthen the planning process, a project wing was set up in November 1983 within the Planning Division of the Finance and Planning Ministry to streamline and improve project appraisal and augment monitoring capability. (A mainframe computer is being acquired to help in the task.) Half-yearly reports of major projects are reviewed by the Executive Committee of the National Economic Council to ensure that any delays or departures from implementation schedules receive top-level attention. Subsequently, the financial limits up to which federal ministries or the higher-level Central Development Working Party can sanction projects have been raised to speed up clearances. Planning and monitoring cells are being set up in all ministries undertaking sizable development programs. Administrative procedures are being changed to bring the Planning Division into the picture at an early stage of the evaluation of major foreign-aided projects to permit quicker approval.

Fifth Plan Progress, Sixth Plan Reforms

Although there has been considerable improvement in the economic environment, further reforms are needed to safeguard and improve the economy's growth potential. This need is recognized in the sixth plan, which calls for improvements in pricing, deregulation, tariffs, import liberalization, and other incentives to induce the private sector to play the larger role assigned to it in major sectors of the economy. The need for reforms has gained urgency in view of further pressure on the balance of payments in the wake of the fall in remittances from Pakistanis working abroad. These transfers have begun to decline because of the downturn in the oil-producing economies of the Middle East, the source of 85 percent of the inflows. This lends added urgency to efforts to reduce the balance of payments gap and to offset the decline in national savings.

The tasks that lie ahead should be seen in the context of the progress that Pakistan has already made in correcting imbalances in its economy. These corrections were not made any easier by the second round of oil price increases in 1979 and the subsequent worldwide recession. Taken together, the rise in oil prices and the recession-induced fall in commodity prices resulted in a decline of Pakistan's terms of trade by 30 percent in 1979–83. On top of this, the crisis in neighboring Afghanistan threw an added burden on the economy despite the humanitarian aid several countries offered to help cope with the influx of refugees. Another major handicap was the cost overrun on some major projects, notably the Tarbela multipurpose dam, which put an added squeeze on resources.

Faced with these difficulties, Pakistan turned to the International Monetary Fund (IMF) in November 1980. A three-year Extended Fund Facility was negotiated, under which the country was able to draw SDR[1] 1,078 million during a two-and-half-year period (the facility was terminated in November 1983 after disagreement on a demand management pro-

1. SDR stands for special drawing right, an international monetary reserve asset created by the International Monetary Fund to supplement existing reserves. It is valued on the basis of five currencies and can be used in a wide variety of transactions and operations among official holders. In October 1985 the value of one SDR was 1.06 dollars.

Aerial view of downtown Karachi, Pakistan's largest city (1985 estimated population: 6.8 million) shows rapid expansion of central business district. Bagh-e-Jinnah is in middle of photograph.

gram for its remaining six months). Nonetheless, the IMF acknowledged that Pakistan's performance was noteworthy on several counts, among them a high rate of economic growth, a balance of payments outcome well above the agreed targets, and substantial progress toward improving both internal and external stabilization through fiscal, exchange rate, and pricing policies.

By 1983, when the fifth plan ended, the budgetary deficit had been reduced to 5.3 percent of GDP, down from 8.5 percent in 1977. During the same period, government borrowings from the domestic banking system had gone down from 4.1 to 1.5 percent of GDP. Monetary growth had slowed from 21.5 to 11.3 percent between 1977 and 1983, and inflation (measured in consumer prices) had been brought down from about 15 to 8.4 percent between 1975 and 1983. The balance of payments showed a current account deficit of 3.1 percent of GNP compared with 6.8 percent in 1977 because of rapid increases in exports and workers' remittances.

The sixth plan has attempted to reflect in its sectoral allocations a new scheme of priorities corresponding to the need for further adjustments in the economy. Accordingly, the share of the total outlay earmarked for energy, water, and the social sector is to increase. Aside from the fertilizer subsidy, which the government has decided to reduce sharply, agriculture has the same share as before in the larger plan outlay. This means a significant increase in allocations in real terms. These changes are to be accommodated by cutting back on industry in the light of the decision to limit the public sector's involvement in this sector.

With resource constraints proving to be greater than anticipated—highlighted by a record budgetary deficit in 1984–85—most of the priority sectors received allocations of funds well short of the plan target in the first two years of the sixth plan. Given the possibility that the resources will continue to fall short of Pakistan's investment goals, it was deemed necessary to identify a core investment program and set clear priorities within each sector. This has been done in a three-year (1985–88) priority investment program to safeguard critical investments. If the three-year program is fully implemented, it should be possible to meet about 90 percent of the overall targets for public sector spending during the five-year period despite the shortfall in the first two years.

The resource constraints underline the need for enlarging public savings. Fixed investment as a proportion of GNP has hardly increased in the past ten years: it was 12 percent in 1973–74 and 12.8 percent in 1983–84. Public investment increased at an annual rate of only 1 percent during the fifth plan. The rate of increase of public and private investment in the aggregate was no more than 2.9 percent in 1978–83. This brings out clearly that high output growth was achieved mainly by running down existing capital assets. The serious deterioration in the physical infrastructure is underlined by the growing level of power shortages in summer months, when hydroelectric generation suffers from a seasonal decline; by the loss of half the gross inflow of water into the irrigation system through seepages and percolation; and by the rundown state of national highways, of which 80 percent have been in need of rehabilitation for some time. The lag in social sector development is reflected in the fact that all relevant indicators show Pakistan much behind other developing countries at a comparable level of per capita income. Enrollment in primary schools for the six-to-eleven age group is only 51 percent, and the rate of adult literacy is only 24 percent. Indicators of the inadequacy of health services are a high rate of infant mortality, 119 per 1,000 live births, and the slow improvement in life expectancy from 43.3 percent in 1960 to 50.2 percent in 1985.

The inability to generate larger budgetary resources is in large part caused by a tax structure which lacks buoyancy. For every 1 percent growth in GNP, the total tax increases by only 1.1 percent, largely through ad hoc measures introduced in the budget each year. The main problem here is the narrow coverage of taxes on domestic production, which contribute 28 percent of tax revenues compared with 36 percent from taxes on imports. The World Bank has strongly recommended introducing a broad sales tax, with the proviso that this tax should be neutral between domestic production and imports to avoid further distortions in the structure of protection.

The resource gap is so large, however, that it cannot be narrowed unless all available avenues for increasing public savings are explored. In particular, charges made to users for services provided by the public sector should be raised to reflect costs and to allow for a return that would permit the utilities to finance their growth themselves to a greater extent than now possible. This applies in particular to water rates farmers pay for irrigation and to charges for electricity for some categories of consumers. Open and implicit subsidies, including the highly expensive subsidy for fertilizers, need to be cut back if not eliminated altogether. Public manufacturing enterprises should be allowed to set market-oriented prices and to improve their operational efficiency. This would free the budget of the burden that it now bears on their account. A 50 percent increase in sales-tax revenue and the elimination of the fertilizer subsidy, for example, would permit the government to double its outlays for the social sectors over the 1984–85 level.

Issues for Future Reform

The impending changes in Pakistan's financial system would eliminate interest and base future transactions on new modes consistent with Islamic principles. The government has repeatedly stressed that changes will be made gradually and cautiously. To the extent that Islamic modes, based intrinsically on the sharing of profits, promote a market-oriented pricing of capital, the shift should enhance the efficiency of financial intermediation. Since the Islamic system is more akin to equity financing, it is possible that it may lead to the diversification of financial instruments to reflect better the opportunity cost of funds. If so, this may stimulate the development of the still embryonic capital market.

Some questions have yet to be resolved. Since Islamic modes of lending increase lenders' risk, this could discourage risk-averse investors. It also remains to be seen what the effect will be on government savings schemes, an important source of funds for the budget. It will all depend on how return on savings is determined under the new dispensation. For its part, the private sector is concerned that funding by public sector financial institutions on an Islamic basis may lead to their involvement in companies' operations. There are indications, however, that borrowers and lenders will set in advance an agreed rate of return. If this is done, the lenders will play no greater role in company operations than they do now.

On a broader level, there is concern that reliance on profit-sharing lending may make it difficult for cyclical industries and long-gestation, capital-intensive projects to obtain finance. The problem may be minimized to the extent that the system operates on the basis of a rate of return agreed to in advance. Complex legal problems are raised by the new financial instruments, and the consensus is that it will be necessary for the judicial system—currently burdened with a heavy backlog of cases—to provide lenders quick redress against defaulting borrowers. The government is considering the creation of special courts for this purpose.

Pakistan, like other developing countries, has to address both the domestic and foreign dimensions of the resource gap. In the context of the latter, it is important to pursue a realistic exchange rate policy because an overvalued rate discourages exports and raises imports and has an adverse effect on such inflows as remittances sent through banking channels. Pakistan has adopted a flexible exchange rate policy since January 1982, when its rupee was delinked from the U.S. dollar and pegged to a basket of currencies. Since then there has been a sizable improvement in export performance, particularly in nontraditional items. The rupee has slowly appreciated again in 1983 and 1984. While a slowdown in exports in 1984–85 was the result largely of unfavorable commodity prices and a weather-related setback to the cotton crop, currency appreciation was undoubtedly also a contributory factor, affecting in particular nontraditional exports to markets such as those in Western Europe.

In sum, Pakistan has to deal with many issues in the context of policy reforms now under way to build a framework for rapid and sustained growth. The main areas in which action needs to be urgently taken are (1) mobilization of larger domestic resources; (2) strengthening international competitiveness through reforms in the structure and degree of protection accorded to domestic producers; (3) improvements in policies and procedures governing new starts in industry, including a shift from administered prices to those reflecting market realities; (4) rationalization of energy prices to promote the development of domestic resources and encourage conservation; and (5) an overhaul of the institutional arrangements and supporting services for agriculture in order to channel a part of future agricultural growth into the production of high-value crops with an export potential.

AGRICULTURE
The Untapped Potential

AGRICULTURE IS THE LIFEBLOOD of Pakistan's economy. Although its relative importance has declined over the past twenty-five years as the result of a development strategy aimed at diversifying the economy, the sector still holds the key to the economy's future. In fact, Pakistan's comparative advantage in certain agricultural and agriculture-based activities implies that the country's economic prospects will remain critically dependent on maintaining and deepening the growth of the farm sector. This will require a strong effort to improve farm yields because there is now very little scope for extending the cropped area.

Back in 1960, agriculture accounted for 46 percent of national GDP; it employed two-fifths of the labor force and contributed three-quarters of exports. Modernization of the economy—both the cause and result of reasonably rapid growth at 6.7 percent in the 1960s and at more than 5 percent since—has altered the economy's structure to a significant extent. But the primacy of agriculture remains unchanged. Its 26 percent share of GDP makes it the largest commodity-producing sector. Its role in employment is still almost as large as it was, with 53 percent of the labor force still dependent on it. Although the share of farm products in total exports has diminished to about 30 percent, another 30 percent consists of textiles and clothing based largely on a bountiful cotton crop.

It is hardly surprising therefore that Pakistan's economy thrives whenever the pace in agriculture picks up—as it has since 1978. The slowdown of the first half of the 1970s is now a thing of the past—as demonstrated by a growth rate of much more than 4 percent achieved in this sector in recent years. This puts Pakistan ahead of most other developing countries in this regard. The point, however, is that the potential for production is far from exhausted. This is one reason why agriculture continues to have priority in the country's plans for sustained growth.

The task that lies ahead is undoubtedly more difficult for three reasons. First, although the sown area has increased as a result of harnessing surface and groundwater resources, there is little scope to extend cultivation any further. Second, Pakistan's population growth rate of 2.7 percent threatens to jeopardize the recent improvement in per capita food output if the growth of production slackens. Third, increasing yields is the only hope of improving incomes in the rural areas, where four-fifths of the population directly depends on agriculture for its livelihood.

The danger in fact in Pakistan is that the cultivated area will shrink because of waterlogging and salinity. Population growth, which accelerated to 3 percent in the past decade, has already worsened the land-population ratio from 200 per square kilometer in 1960 to 324 in 1980. There is now a strong compulsion to get more out of each hectare of land to maintain, if not improve, food balance and farm incomes, as well as provide the raw materials needed for the continued growth of agro-based industry and the generation of surpluses for export.

The Effort to Increase Yields

The importance of improving productivity can scarcely be overstated. It is only in the 1980s that Pakistan has achieved self-sufficiency in wheat, its staple food, and sugar, although it had become a net exporter of food several years earlier because of a surge in rice output. Imports which sustained consumption in the past—wheat accounted for about 12 percent of the import bill in the early 1970s—will mean a heavier sacrifice than before. With export earnings sufficient now to pay for only about 45 percent of imports compared with about 65 percent before the oil price explosion of 1973, there is much less scope for maneuver.

The social and political importance of increasing yields must be stressed. For the 71 percent of the population living in rural areas, there can be little hope otherwise of improving incomes. This is all the more true now because farm prices in Pakistan have over the years been raised to a level equal to, or in excess of, international prices for such major crops as wheat, high-yielding varieties of rice, and sugar. Because subsidies to agriculture, in the form of underpriced water and fertilizer, are much in excess of the direct revenues obtained from the sector, there is little that the government, facing severe resource constraints, can do for farmers except to help them help themselves by increasing the harvest they garner from their fields.

Yields of Pakistan's major crops have indeed increased, but these have been one-time improvements following the introduction of new seeds or improved access to water. For instance, the yield of wheat rose at an annual rate of 6.2 percent and of rice at 4.8 percent in 1965–70. Subsequent improvement in wheat has been no more than about 3 percent a year, while there has been virtual stagnation in sugarcane. Yield growth for the other major crops has been slow.

There are two pointers to improved yields. A comparison with other similarly placed countries shows how far behind Pakistan still is despite its revived agricultural growth in recent years. In wheat, Pakistan's yield in 1983 was about 9 percent lower than India's and Turkey's and 54 percent lower than Egypt's. Paddy yields were about 20 percent less than the Asian average and 60 percent less than in Korea. In seed cotton, Pakistani yields were only one-third of those obtained by Egypt and Turkey. Sugarcane showed a similar difference—the Pakistani level was lower than in India and less than half of the all-Asian average.

An even better indicator of the potential which Pakistan has so far failed to realize is the evidence of fertility trials carried out within the country in farmers' fields. A 1981–82 report from the Department of Agriculture in Punjab showed that improved farm practices, particularly the optimum use of fertilizer, would increase yields by 28 percent to almost 100 percent for different crops including unirrigated wheat. Better farmers in Pakistan are indeed getting such results, which suggests that the average can grow appreciably if others are helped, and perhaps prodded, to do a better job of farming their plots.

What needs to be done is well understood in Pakistan because of the work done by its own experts as well as by international agencies. The broad direction was mapped out in the National Agricultural Policy adopted in 1980. This was followed by the completion of major studies on irrigated agriculture financed by the U.N. Development Programme and executed by the World Bank. The fact that agricultural growth improved from 2.3 percent during the fourth five-year plan (1973–74 to 1977–78) to 4.4 percent in the subsequent plan period was in part the result of good weather. Policy changes also made an unmistakable contribution. The task Pakistan is now addressing is to consolidate the improvement through better and stronger implementation of these policies. Its efforts are being reinforced by the international agencies, notably the World Bank, and bilateral aid.

An indicator of the importance Pakistan attaches to the task is the increase envisaged in development expenditures in the agricultural sector during the current five-year plan covering 1983–84 to 1987–88. Even allowing for inflation, expenditure is targeted to increase about 50 percent more than in the previous plan. Although outlays may be constrained by financial stringency, the scope for new initiatives is still quite large because a decision to reduce the fertilizer subsidy should free budgetary resources thus preempted. In addition, some of the tasks that the government has hitherto

Students at tractor school in Lahore learn to use and maintain farm machinery. World Bank lending has enabled Pakistan to increase the use of tractors in farming.

undertaken will be shared by the private sector now that policies have shifted to favor greater private participation in the distribution of inputs backed by the provision of extension services, agroprocessing, storage, and marketing. The plan makes the assumption that private investment in agriculture will be 220 percent higher in nominal terms (about 135 percent in real terms) than in the previous plan. In view of the financial constraints that Pakistan is facing, the actual increase may fall short of the targets in this case too.

This underlines the need for improvements in the efficiency of investment and for getting the priorities right to ensure that available resources are allocated in a manner that will yield the maximum benefit. The four major crops—wheat, cotton, rice, and sugarcane, accounting for nearly 60 percent of the GDP of the agriculture sector and at least 80 percent of cropped acreage—qualify for the highest attention.

There is no gainsaying that the prices of what farmers buy and sell are important in getting them to put their best foot forward. Since the establishment of the Agricultural Prices Commission in 1981, the government has had the benefit of its recommendations in formulating well-conceived and timely price policies. The task is all the more important now in view of the commitments made to phase out the fertilizer subsidy and to move toward realistic charges for water. Meeting these commitments when the government has little scope for raising support prices will require using price changes to induce efficiency. Particular attention will have to be paid to improvements in marketing to give the farmer a higher proportion of the final consumer price and to reduce the spread between the landed costs of imports and what the farmer has to pay. The marketing costs at both ends are currently high and tending to rise. Moreover, Pakistan is now seeking to give agriculture a stronger export orientation. Besides emphasizing such traditional export items as rice and raw cotton, the hope is to develop markets in nearby Middle Eastern countries for vegetables, fruit, beef, and poultry. This will require fine-tuning support prices to ensure that Pakistan can build up exports with a minimal reliance on subsidies. It will also be necessary to keep a close watch on changes in international markets in determining domestic price policies of the main commodities.

Improved utilization of inputs is the key to the growth of production and an increase in yields. Fertilizer is no doubt the most important; the sixth plan assumes that 48 percent of the increase in major crop output will come from larger and better use of fertilizers. Water is expected to contribute another 16 percent. These approximations may be valid on the basis of past experience, but an improvement in cultural practices to make the most of these inputs may yield a better aggregate result. Because farm-level knowledge of the right practices is limited, there is a need for effective adaptive research and extension work.

Pakistan has made a considerable investment in developing extension services, but the devastation of the cotton crop in 1983 by pests shows how much remains to be done. Activities need to be commodity-specific, field-based, and targeted at small farmers. A third of the area under cultivation is in farms of fewer than five hectares. It will be difficult to improve the overall productivity of Pakistani agriculture unless an increasing number of small farmers perform better.

The use of inputs, particularly by small farmers, depends on the availability of credit. Pakistan has introduced several institutional mechanisms—for example, a lending guideline for commercial banks requiring them to allocate a proportion of their new lending to farmers. The results are still uneven: only 5 percent of institutional credit is going to tenant farmers. The government has recently taken measures to ensure that the impressive increase in the quantity of credit is accompanied by an improvement in its distribution and effectiveness. The system of supervised credit instituted by the Agricultural Development Bank of Pakistan, which attempts to combine credit with guidance in its use, deserves to be extended.

A wider use of adequate inputs will undoubtedly help to improve average yields, but there cannot be sustained progress unless steps are taken to augment supplies and improve quality. Seeds are a case in point. In Punjab, Pakistan's granary, the distribution of certified seeds met only 10 percent of the requirements for wheat and 60 percent for cotton. The number of seed-processing plants must increase to make rapid multiplication possible, a task in which the private sector is now being invited to participate more fully. Likewise, plant protection cannot be really effective without an adequate surveillance and early-warning system. The first step toward this was recently taken with the establishment of emergency centers to safeguard the cotton and rice crops.

Although Pakistan is a labor-surplus economy, particularly in the rural sector where underemployment is a marked feature, there is nevertheless a need for some modest steps toward farm mechanization. The sixth plan envisages the introduction of 50,000 medium-size and small tractors a year; these are undoubtedly needed for raising cropping intensity, deepening and improving tillage, and speeding farm operations to allow time for raising a second crop. But small farmers with limited resources cannot share in these benefits unless some institutional arrangements are made with them specifically in mind.

The World Bank's Role

Historically, the World Bank has placed special emphasis on lending for agriculture. The Bank and the government are in agreement on the main elements of a strategy which underpins lending in this sector. In recent years, the objective has been to increase agricultural productivity by improving the efficiency of the irrigation system and supporting agricultural services. Among the issues being addressed are the balance between short-gestation projects and longer-term expenditures, rationalization of input and output prices, marketing, improvements in operation and maintenance, cost recovery, and a wider role for the private sector.

Of the $3.2 billion World Bank lending to Pakistan (through June 30, 1985), approximately 30 percent has been for agriculture and irrigation. In the past five years, the biggest portion of the Bank's assistance for the agricultural sector (excluding irrigation) has gone to the Agricultural Development Bank of Pakistan in support of its lending program. The amount made available in the past five years was approximately $88 million. The second largest share of the Bank's assistance has been for research and extension; loans made in the past five years totaled approximately $54 million. In these extension projects, the executing agencies were provincial governments, with the result that they too participated in the policy dialogue.

A third category of loans has been for such needs as the promotion of dairying and forestry, improvements in grain storage, the development of edible oil crops, and the establishment of facilities for seed breeding and multiplication.

IRRIGATION
The Quest for Productivity

LESS THAN ONE-FIFTH of the water the Pakistani farmer uses in growing crops comes from precipitation. The rest comes from surface irrigation and groundwater brought up by pumping. There would not be a significant agriculture sector in the arid country but for the effort invested in harnessing water from the mighty Indus River and its tributaries on the one hand and from underground aquifers charged by rain and seepage from watercourses on the other.

More than 90 percent of the value of Pakistan's agricultural production comes from irrigated land. Irrigation in the Indus Plain began more than 5,000 years ago. The present-day network of headworks, barrages, and canals began to be built under British auspices in the late 1800s. There are today three major reservoirs with a storage capacity of 18,500 million cubic meters, nineteen barrages and headworks, forty-three canal commands through which run 57,200 kilometers of canals, and another 1.6 million kilometers of water courses and field channels. In addition, more than 200,000 wells supply almost half as much water as that received in the fields from canals. To a depth of forty meters, 47 percent of the Indus Basin has groundwater of a quality acceptable for irrigation. Pakistan depends on this network for 90 percent of its total agricultural value.

This vast irrigation network serving 14 million hectares is the largest contiguous system in the world. Pakistan can also claim the distinction of having the world's largest earthwork dam, Tarbela, which became operational in 1977. Within each of the 43 canal commands, there are numerous lower-order commands. The lowest level, called *chak*, ranging in size from 80 to 280 hectares, covers twenty to fifty farms with an average size of 35 hectares. A collectively maintained channel brings water from the government-owned and -operated canal to the chak. Within it, the watercourses are built and maintained individually. Distribution within a chak is by a time rotation called *warabandi*, with each farm allotted a specific time period in proportion to its size. The allocation of water within the chak, arrived at through consultations among the beneficiary farmers, is supervised by the provincial irrigation department.

Problems of the Irrigation Network

The huge size of the Pakistani network means, however, that its problems are equally large. The amount of water diverted into canals has led to so much seepage that the water table in areas with inadequate drainage has risen alarmingly over the years. According to a 1981 survey, 22 percent of the Indus Basin has water within 1.8 meters of the surface and 42 percent within 3 meters. According to the findings of an earlier survey, the problem was only half as acute in 1953. Moreover, soils in areas subject to waterlogging—15 to 40 percent of canal command areas during various periods of the year— suffer from salinity. This has resulted in a decline in yields over substantial areas and the total cessation of cultivation in the worst-hit pockets. About 8 percent of the cultivated acreage is now classified as highly saline. Another 6 percent is moderately affected. The incidence is greater in the lower basin.

Pakistan has no choice but to overhaul its system of water management to deal with these severe problems. At the same time, it must endeavor to increase the amount of water actually delivered to the farmers to permit them to intensify cropping. Many can raise only one crop in a year with the water they now get. With a worsening land-population ratio, the growth of the agricultural sector is critically dependent on raising crop intensity. Since two-thirds of the water flowing through the Indus system is already being diverted into canals, there is not much room for drawing in additional supplies. The emphasis must therefore fall on making better use of the water already harnessed by the system by addressing two main tasks. One is to cut the large losses because of deep percolation and evaporation—some 25 percent of the flow through the canals. The second is to ensure that the water delivered to the fields is put to the most productive use. Only 40 to 50 percent of the water reaches the root-zone crops—while 65 percent is thought to be attainable with better water management on farms. Pakistan cannot afford these losses, which amount to half the gross inflow into the system. Water was always a scarce resource in the country, but it is becoming even more so with a broadening and deepening of the agricultural base to meet growing needs and to tap the potential of export markets.

The problems Pakistan faces are, in a sense, a historical legacy. The irrigation system was designed to cover the maximum possible area and spread the flow to the largest number of farmers. Crop intensity was not an objective at a time when the population was smaller and its growth quite slow. As a result, canals were long and thus had high maintenance and operation costs. Most of the channels through which water flows are unlined, and no provision was made in their design or operation to combat silting. This limits the volume of water that can be carried today and places various constraints on meeting the requirements of crops in time—a grave handicap because modern inputs (seeds and fertilizers) require reliable supplies of water to fulfill their promise. Moreover, the less the assurance of timely and adequate supplies of water, the greater is the farmer's resistance to paying realistic water charges and using an economically optimum level of inputs.

Historically, the canals have been operated by the government, while watercourses and field channels have been maintained by beneficiaries under informal arrangements that have evolved over time. Until recently, there has been little effort to improve on these arrangements to ensure better maintenance or bring about technical changes to mitigate losses. Moreover, the pattern of water use through a weekly rotation of water among beneficiaries, with time slots graded according to the size of landholdings, does not necessarily correspond with the watering regime of the new crops.

It is now obvious, not only to administrators but also to the beneficiaries, that the whole system is badly run down, despite larger allocations for developing and maintaining water resources. The sixth five-year plan's investment program of Rs32 billion for the water sector is 104 percent higher in current prices than the fifth plan's. Because of the need to protect and improve the irrigation system, the largest allocations and greatest share increases have gone to drainage, reclamation, and irrigation. Yet resources set apart for maintenance of the system fall short of requirements; an important contributory factor is the ever-widening gap between revenues collected for water charges and the irrigation operating and maintenance costs.

In a welcome shift of priorities, provincial governments, which are in charge of operation and maintenance, are increasing their budgets for this purpose. This is in recognition of the need for a better balance among investment in new facilities, rehabilitation of an aging system, and maintenance expenditures. A problem here is the division of responsibility between provincial governments and the federal government. With limited financial capacity and inadequate incentives, provinces have often allocated insufficient funds to priority projects in order to obtain additional federal assistance. In addition, the interprovincial apportionment of Indus waters has not been finally settled. The present system of ad hoc distribution results in suboptimal use of surface and groundwater supplies. Provinces have been slow to concede actual water losses from their networks and have instead been press-

Watercourse and leveling at farm water management project in Thal, Punjab Province. Project was assisted by World Bank.

ing the federal government for major additions to the system. This bid to raise the level of water use is an attempt to establish a claim for a higher share whenever the issue of water rights is eventually decided.

Sixth Plan Tasks

Pakistan has set itself three tasks under its sixth plan. The first task is to protect fertile lands from waterlogging, salinity, and flooding. This calls for the completion of remedial work on the Tarbela Dam to improve the hydraulic behavior of canal systems adversely affected by it. Begun in the second half of the 1970s, this work is nearing completion. With fewer resources now preempted by it, the availability of more money for other parts of the program should help to accelerate progress. A major effort is being made to provide drainage in areas subject to severe waterlogging—areas underlain with saline groundwater. Two-fifths of the targeted plan outlays are earmarked for this purpose.

This emphasis is not new; drainage and reclamation have claimed the largest share of budgetary resources devoted to water in the past twenty years. What is new, however, is that the responsibility for a large part of the task is being transferred to the private sector. In areas where groundwater is suitable for irrigation, the government will step back and let the private sector develop tubewells to provide both drainage and additional irrigation. Incentives to the private sector include the provision of electricity, credit facilities, and the tubewell subsidy. The government will, therefore, be able to concentrate its resources on the drainage of areas in which subsurface water is saline and there is thus no incentive for individual farmers to draw it up for use in their fields.

The second task identified in the plan is to improve the irrigation system along lines set out in 1975 in a master plan drawn up in collaboration with the World Bank. The proposed investment options have been evaluated with the use of modeling techniques devised by the World Bank's Development Research Department. By taking into account both surface and groundwater resources, the plan outlines options in terms of the agricultural production that these will yield.

The system is to be improved by remodeling canals to increase their delivery capability and reduce losses en route. This large task will be carried out over many years and will be combined with rehabilitation work on canals and improvement of water courses—all with the object of improving efficiency and husbanding available water. More than a quarter of the plan allocation for water is earmarked for these endeavors.

The handicap of limited resources has made it all the more necessary to undertake the third task in the plan—organizational and managerial changes to enhance the benefits. A major initiative in this direction is a World Bank–aided project to upgrade the management of the irrigation system at the command level by developing techniques and programs suitable for a wide range of agroclimatic conditions. This will require some improvements in the physical infrastructure, but the focus will be on combining better delivery of water with its more efficient use by ensuring the supply of other inputs and services required for increased agricultural production. Included in the project is a pilot program to introduce water charges related to the volume of water actually delivered to a farmer's field. At present, charges have no direct relationship to the quantity supplied, with the result that there is no incentive for efficient use.

This experiment gains added interest from the fact that Pakistan has been raising water charges with the object of achieving full recovery of costs in all provinces by 1992. At present, the gap between costs and recovery is about 50 percent, and the water charge accounts for no more than 6 percent of the income from crops. As water supplies become more reliable as a result of physical and managerial changes, it will be easier to gain acceptance for higher charges.

Farmers too will have to do their part to achieve an overall improvement of the system. The watercourses which they are responsible for building and maintaining lose more than half the water coming through them to the fields (as established by a sample survey). Available methods of reducing water loss would cost only 25 percent of what would be required to develop new sources for an equivalent volume. In recognition of this potential for saving, Pakistan embarked on a pilot project in 1976 with help from the U.S. Agency for International Development (USAID) to improve on-farm water management by improving watercourses, leveling land to facilitate the distribution of water, and organizing water users' associations to ensure better maintenance in the future. The encouraging results—reflected in the enthusiastic response from farmers, who supplied all the unskilled labor required for civil works—has led to the adoption of projects to bring about similar improvements in a much wider area.

The World Bank's Role

The World Bank has been deeply involved in Pakistan's irrigation program for many years. It provided its good offices for the country's negotiations with India for a treaty determining the allocation of Indus waters between the co-riparian nations. The treaty was signed in 1960 and was backed by an Indus Basin Development Fund of $800 million contributed by friendly countries to compensate for the flow diverted to India. This fund, as well as a subsequent fund of $1.2 billion for building the Tarbela Dam, were administered by the Bank.

In the past five years, the Bank has continued to help with important tasks for harnessing and managing water resources—salinity control and reclamation, drainage, rehabilitation, improvement in water management at the command and farm levels, and groundwater development. In the last-named field, the Bank is particularly interested in supporting Pakistan's decision to tap private initiatives and capital to the fullest extent. In line with the division of responsibilities in Pakistan, the Bank is working on maintenance and rehabilitation projects with all four provincial governments. The projects for improved management at the command and farm level also fall within the jurisdiction of the provinces. Since major additions or changes to physical facilities are undertaken by the federal government, assistance for such projects is directed to it. The eighteen projects that the World Bank assisted between 1978 and 1985 received Bank loans totaling almost $1 billion.

The first On-Farm Water Management Project, financed by a $41 million IDA credit, was approved in 1982 and received cofinancing from the International Fund for Agricultural Development. In 1985, IDA approved another credit of $34.5 million to consolidate the gains of this first project. Among the objectives of the second On-Farm Water Management Project were to reduce irrigation water losses at the farm level, increase agricultural production through more efficient use of water, and increase farmer participation in water users' associations in order to improve the management of water and other farm inputs.

The World Bank has played and is playing a principal role in meeting Pakistan's needs from 1984 to 1988 in support of Pakistan's sixth plan programs. Apart from the help that the Bank itself may provide, it will also seek to harness additional funds from governmental and private sources to facilitate the implementation of the plans that Pakistan has adopted for developing and safeguarding its precious water resource.

Pakistan's development plans acknowledge that in order to increase yields and production, investments in drainage, rehabilitation, and water management must be accompanied by measures to address the other aspects of agriculture. There is a need to strengthen agricultural support services, to maintain appropriate input and output prices, to strengthen irrigation and agricultural institutions, and to widen the role of the private sector (including the privatization of groundwater development).

POWER
The Battle against Shortages

LIKE MANY DEVELOPING COUNTRIES, Pakistan is faced with increasing shortages of power. During periods when seasonal factors reduce generation, a quarter or more of the demand cannot be met by the available supply. The demand-supply gap is likely to persist for the rest of the decade, chiefly because of investment constraints. The overall problem stemming from a low rate of national savings has been aggravated by policies which inhibit greater participation of domestic and foreign private capital in developing energy resources. The task in the power sector is therefore twofold. First, shortages must be mitigated through improved efficiency in generation, distribution, and consumption. Realistic pricing can make an important contribution to the endeavor by giving incentives for more economical consumption. Second, a strategy for power development must be evolved that will yield the maximum output at the least cost and hold down the bill for imported energy resources in a country with an already large trade deficit.

Of the total commercial energy used in Pakistan, amounting to just over 16 million tons of oil equivalent in 1983–84, more than 30 percent was consumed in the form of electricity. The growth rate of electricity consumption has significantly accelerated in recent years—from 6.6 percent a year in 1973–

78 to 11.3 percent in 1978–83—partly as a result of pricing policies devised to shift demand for energy away from imported oil. As a result, electricity consumption per thousand rupees of GDP rose from 170 kilowatt-hours (kWh) in 1973 to 236 kWh in 1983—an increase of 3.3 percent a year in the intensity of use. The elasticity of consumption in relation to GDP increased from 1.3 in 1973–78 to 1.9 in 1978–83. Consumption per capita, net of system losses, has increased from 90 to 158 kWh. Notwithstanding these increases, both the elasticity and per capita consumption are modest in comparison with the average for low-income countries of South and East Asia.

The Consumption Pattern

Industry takes up a little less than two-fifths of the power supply from utilities. In addition, industry draws on its own captive capacity of about 430 megawatts (MW), or 8.5 percent of the total for utilities. More than a quarter of the supply goes to residential customers and just over a sixth to agriculture. The number of households connected to electricity has grown from 1.5 million in 1973 to 3.9 million in 1983 (to one out of every three households in the country). This sharp rise has been facilitated by a pricing policy which has kept the increase in charges for domestic consumption well below the rate of inflation. Another notable feature is a surge in the use of household appliances, which is explained in part by imports made by returning emigrants.

The growth of industrial consumption, admittedly from an already large base, has been about 11 percent a year in recent years, compared with the sharp increase of 23 percent in the residential sector, 15 percent in commercial establishments, and 8 percent in agriculture. It is likely that growth in industrial demand would have been higher but for the supply constraints highlighted by restrictions on consumption during periods when peak demand exceeded available capacity. Industrial consumers bear the brunt of measures to conserve supplies—for example, a reduction in shifts from three to two to ease the situation in the peak demand period. Broadly speaking, just over a quarter of the energy used in industry is in the form of electricity—compared with a share of three-quarters in agriculture and two-fifths among households.

Sources of Power

More than half of Pakistan's total 1983–84 generating capacity of 5,100 MW was in units utilizing the water flows of the Indus River system. The share of fossil fuels was more than two-fifths, while a nuclear power plant in Karachi accounted for the residual balance of less than 3 percent. Of fossil fuels, natural gas was by far the most important, with a two-thirds share in all fuel consumption. Except for a share of less than half a percent taken by coal, oil accounted for the rest. Only five years earlier, gas was almost the only fossil fuel used for generation, with a share of as much as 98 percent. The very sharp subsequent increase in the share of oil—both fuel oil for large units and diesel oil for small, isolated ones—reflects a slowdown in the growth of gas supplies because pricing policies held back exploration and development. In the five years since 1978, consumption of gas for power generation increased by only 10 percent a year compared with an explosive growth of 227 percent for fuel oil and 82 percent for diesel. Since Pakistan is heavily dependent on imports for its oil consumption, this development puts a serious strain on the balance of payments.

Hydroelectric Power Potential

Pakistan has large energy resources, chief among them being the hydroelectric power potential of four rivers—the Chinab, Indus, Jhelum, and Kabul. Plants of 100 to 2,000 MW could generate in theory as much as 30,000 MW, the bulk of it at upstream locations in the north. On the basis of present technology and relative prices, the economically feasible potential so far identified amounts to almost 17,000 MW. Of this, about 18 percent has been developed or is under construction. The Water and Power Development Authority (WAPDA), the agency chiefly responsible for power development, has highly ambitious plans to harness another 8,500 MW during the next two decades. What is lacking is an inventory of sites with smaller potential of up to 50 MW. Investigations to develop technical and cost data for such sites will be useful in rounding out long-term plans. Cost is going to be a major constraint on increases in capacity; the dual-purpose dam project to be built on the Indus at Kalabagh to raise 1,200 MW in each of the first two stages extending up to 1998 is likely to require more than $5 billion at today's prices and substantially more to achieve its full potential of 3,600 MW. The next one further upstream at Basha, which is ranked as the second most attractive site and may yield another 2,400 MW, is estimated to cost $3 billion. This is, however, only a preliminary figure.

There are two problems with hydroelectric power. First, there are seasonal fluctuations in flows. There is little rain from October to May, when the demand on reservoirs for irrigation water is high. The effective capability of the hydroelectric units is sharply reduced in these months. From the water level at the height of the wet season to the bottom of the trough in dry months, the drop can be as much as 45 percent. Second, the storage capacity of the reservoirs is getting reduced by the silt being brought into them by river flows. It is now clear that corrective measures have to be undertaken to improve the hydrological regime and minimize the problem.

The Untapped Potential of Energy Minerals

After water, the next-largest energy resources are natural gas and oil. The role of gas in power generation is diminishing as a result of supply constraints. An alternative to oil now being investigated is domestic and imported coal. Pakistan produced 1.7 million tons of coal in 1984, equivalent to 0.7 million tons of oil equivalent, or less than a quarter of current consumption. Only a fraction of this is as yet used for power

Iqbal town power station in Lahore, built with World Bank assistance.

generation at a small (15 MW) plant at Quetta. There seems to be scope for doing much more despite the serious problems of a high ash and sulfur content. Reserves in the coal and lignite fields in the Quetta area, in the Salt range in northern Punjab, and around Hyderabad in Sind are estimated at 835 million tons, of which only 107 are proven. Many possibly coal-bearing areas remain unexplored, suggesting that reserves may be substantially higher—perhaps 1,200 million tons. Almost half the present production comes from the Lakrah field in Sind, which could support a power plant of 300

MW capacity. Studies are in progress with funds from the World Bank and USAID to assess reserves and to identify operational problems and ways to resolve them. Parallel work is being undertaken on the economics of a power complex at Karachi using imported coal. As part of the same exercise, the potential for increased private investment in coal is also being examined to develop a model framework to be applied first to Lakrah and later to other promising areas. The working of the Pakistan Mineral Development Corporation, the public agency that accounts for 15 percent of current production, is also being examined to see whether its high cost of production can be reduced.

Indigenous uranium is already being used for power generation at the nuclear power plant in Karachi, which still operates at well below its rated capacity of 125 MW. The presence of uranium in the sandstones of Dera Ghazikhan has been known for some time, and there are indications of occurrences in the Potwar area near Islamabad. The Pakistan Atomic Energy Commission is currently exploring two reasonably large reserves, which may prove sufficient to provide uranium fuel for a relatively sizable nuclear power program in the future. At present, the only estimate of uranium resources dates from 1976, when the reserves with a cutoff rate of 0.1 percent uranium oxide were estimated at 150,000 tons (metric) of mineralized material containing about 180 tons of uranium metal.

The Optimal Strategy

Recognizing that power shortages are putting a brake on economic growth, Pakistan is undertaking a series of measures to get more out of its existing capacity and improve the efficiency of its consumption. At the same time, an effort is being made to step up investment in new capacity in the context of studies now in hand to define a path of development that will cost the least in the long run. Power generation and distribution now account for almost two-thirds of the overall investment in energy and one-fifth of all public investment.

Although the claim on resources may continue to be large, a well-conceived strategy will ensure optimal allocation and timing of investments within the power subsector.

Since any plan for investment is subject to uncertainties about the availability of resources, Pakistan has no choice but to identify a core investment program based on a careful study of priorities and foreign-exchange financing committed or in the pipeline. This program includes new generating capacity to be completed during the current plan period and preparatory work on units—hydroelectric as well as thermal—to come into operation by 1990. This is expected to add 1,660 MW of capacity by about mid-1988 and 2,740 MW by 1990. Also included in the program are major transmission lines of 500 and 220 kilovolts (kV) to upgrade facilities for a nationwide interchange of power between hydropower installations in the north and principal load centers and thermal plants in the rest of the country. This is necessary to rationalize generation by making greater use of low-cost units to meet the base load and to save on standby capacity required for coping with outage or maintenance shutdowns.

The upgrading of transmission should help to mitigate losses that now occur in the system because of excessive length and the loading of relatively low voltage lines of 66 and 132 kV. As of 1973, losses in transmission as a percentage of net generation amounted to 9.7 percent in the WAPDA system; this accounts for more than four-fifths of electricity sales in Pakistan. Further losses in distribution from substations to final consumers were much larger—about 20 percent of the net supply discounted for transmission losses. The aggregate loss was thus 29.7 percent. Though this was lower than in the past, the level is about twice as high as the optimal level of 15 percent. (The optimal level is based on the experience of systems with similar configuration in the geographical spread of consumption). Although Pakistan is now apportioning 40 percent of its investments on power for transmission and distribution, corresponding to international norms, a higher share may be appropriate in view of the high losses. For instance, some parts of the distribution network are fifty years old and hence urgently need replacement.

Pricing Policy

Along with reducing losses, there is a need to rationalize consumption to make available capacity go further. Until 1982, Pakistan was pursuing a policy designed to protect the economy from the rising cost of imported oil. While an adjustment in the price of natural gas is under way, the reform of the electricity tariff has not made much progress. As of June 1984, the weighted average of WAPDA was Rs0.64 per kWh, which recovered only 60 percent of the average long-term marginal costs. In addition, tariffs varied by category of consumer but did not reflect the differences in supply costs or in the economic value of power to different users. In particular, the price to residential consumers is in real terms only two-thirds of what it was in 1973, whereas that charged to all other categories of consumers has increased. By 1983, this increase was 13 percent for agricultural users (another preferred category) and 39 percent for industrial users. Despite such modest increases, WAPDA was able to finance more than 40 percent of its investment program from internally generated resources. (This figure does not take into account the fact that WAPDA does not incur any capital costs for the hydroelectric projects at Tarbela and Mangla, which contributed 70 percent of the total electricity generated in 1984.) In view of the heavy maintenance and capital expenditures that lie ahead, WAPDA will need to have additional revenues of its own apart from what a tight federal budget can provide. In revising tariffs, WAPDA will need to consider charging a realistic price to larger domestic consumers, although low-income consumers using limited amounts of power may continue to be offered a concessional price on social grounds. It is also necessary to consider whether prices charged to industry should be uniform or differentiated by value added. A study of costs and benefits of differential pricing should be part of a review of the system's load and management. Consideration may also have to be given to time-of-day metering of consumption for consumers other than those on low-voltage supplies because of the big differences between costs of generation in peak and off-peak periods. Such differential pricing was advocated in a 1979–80 study undertaken by WAPDA.

Realistic pricing will stimulate energy conservation. According to a recent study by USAID, energy conservation investments of about $300 million could yield annual savings of $200 million. Some important initiatives have already been undertaken—for instance, the conversion of cement plants from wet to dry process to reduce energy consumption per unit of output. These plants were simultaneously required to change from natural gas to fuel oil to release gas for higher-value uses. The government is now taking steps to establish an energy conservation center in the Ministry of Planning. Under the auspices of the center, energy audits are to take place—first in public industries to assess the potential for savings in consumption.

It is recognized that changes are necessary in the quality and style of management of public energy enterprises. The lack of financial and managerial autonomy is a main obstacle in the search for better operational efficiency. The government is considering separating the function of generating power from the responsibility for distribution, which may be handed over to agencies set up by provinces or in the private sector. The government also has no objection to industries adding to their captive generating capacities; one idea is to promote industrial estates, whose tenants could get together to set up plants to meet their needs. Steps have been taken to improve energy planning by setting up an office in the Ministry of Planning mandated to collect, compile, and analyze data which would be used to formulate long-term plans to identify priorities and evaluate resource requirements.

The World Bank's Role

Over the years, the World Bank has made a significant contribution to Pakistan's power development. The Bank has worked in conjunction with other donors on a major program to develop the water resources of the Indus Basin for the twofold purpose of providing irrigation and generating power. This included the hydroelectric plants at Mangla and Tarbela, which together account for 83 percent of the country's total hydroelectric generation capacity. Since 1970, the Bank's involvement has been more directly in support of the government's program to upgrade the power transmission and distribution systems.

Of the $3.2 billion that the World Bank has committed to Pakistan, 14 percent has been devoted to energy, including power. Lending for energy has expanded rapidly since 1981–82 as part of a broad exercise to help the Pakistani economy undertake structural adjustments to cope with a changing international environment.

Under a $140 million structural adjustment loan, funds were made available for a number of detailed studies of long-term energy planning that included power development within their broad framework. These have been followed by a $178 million loan in 1985 for the energy sector to finance important investments during the next two years in power generation, transmission, and distribution; the assessment and development of coal resources; and energy conservation.

The Bank is assisting both WAPDA and the partly privately owned Karachi Electric Supply Corporation, which undertakes generation and distribution in and around the city to augment capacity and strengthen transmission facilities. A $100 million Bank loan approved in 1985 is assisting expansion of WAPDA's power transmission systems; this is the fifth project supported by the Bank under an expansion program started in 1970.

As important as financing is the search for better policies to ensure that available funds are used to the best advantage. The World Bank is assisting Pakistan in the search by participating in technical studies and consultations to refine the options. As a result of these exchanges, Pakistan has initiated work on long-term planning to map out an optimal, least-cost development strategy. A plan embodying this strategy is

to be completed by the end of 1986. Studies have also been
started to identify reasons for energy losses and to develop
plans for investments as well as operational improvements
to minimize the losses.

OIL AND GAS
The Search for New Resources

PAKISTAN'S CONSUMPTION of hydrocarbons—divided almost equally between oil and gas—constitutes almost three-quarters of its primary energy requirements. Natural gas is a domestic resource, but the bulk of oil is imported, preempting more than half the country's export earnings. The task is to reduce this import bill. There is, therefore, an urgent need to increase the domestic production of both gas and oil to keep pace with energy consumption, which is growing at more than 8 percent a year. If consumption continues to outpace increases in domestic supply, balance of payments constraints may result in severe shortages of energy to the detriment of economic growth.

The oil bill for crude and products together has risen sharply in recent years from $611 million in 1979 to $1,463 million in 1985, an increase of 19 percent a year. This is because the growth of natural gas output has slowed since 1980 and was almost stagnant in 1984, which compelled the government to require some power plants and the cement industry to use fuel oil in place of gas. The slowdown is not because Pakistan is running out of recoverable reserves but because unattractive prices, which have now been revised, led to a slackening in exploration and development. The oil investment framework is flexible and appropriate, but the tendency in the past was to reserve large areas of exploration and development for the Oil and Gas Development Corporation (OGDC), a public agency with limited technical and labor resources. Following a review of policies regarding both oil and gas, changes are under way to ease these constraints to promote a vigorous search for indigenous hydrocarbons.

Both oil and gas are used throughout the economy, but their relative importance varies from sector to sector. Transport depends solely on oil and has little scope for interfuel substitution in the foreseeable future. Gas has a decided edge in the power sector: out of the 41 percent of power output based on fossil fuels, the share of gas is 70 percent and of oil 29 percent. In industry, gas is again the largest single source, with a share of 40 percent; oil contributes 14 and coal 17 percent. The role of oil and gas is actually larger since electricity, which meets 29 percent of industry's energy needs, is generated partly with these fossil fuels. Within the industry sector, fertilizer output depends solely on gas. More than a fifth of agriculture's energy needs are met by oil and the balance by electricity. In the household sector, gas and oil have an equal share of 29 percent each while the balance is contributed almost entirely by electricity.

Although the potential for using imported coal to replace fuel oil in industry concentrated in and around Karachi is being examined in the context of using coal for power generation in that region, oil and gas will continue to be the predominant fossil fuels for as long as one can foresee. This is why the effort to locate domestic sources of these fuels merits the highest priority.

The Search for Oil

Since 1915, oil has been produced in the Potwar Basin just south of Islamabad and processed at a small refinery at Attock (which has a current capacity of more than 30,000 barrels a day, or about 1.5 million metric tons a year). Although the potential for expanding production through further exploration in the basin was well known, little effort was made to do so until 1976 because of difficult drilling conditions, low international prices before the escalation that began in 1973, and a lack of incentives to draw foreign companies into an area with modest prospects by world standards. In the thirty years from independence to 1977, in all of Pakistan only 160 exploration and development wells were drilled by foreign oil companies and 30 by OGDC. Exploration by foreign oil companies in this period reached a peak in 1958 as a result of a spurt following the discovery of large gas deposits at Sui in Baluchistan in 1952. Since the results of the subsequent search were not too encouraging, exploration dropped sharply after 1960.

In 1976, the government adopted new legislation to stimulate private exploration. This set a limit of 55 percent on the government's share in gross profits, offered concessionary duties on the importing of equipment, and assured repatriation of net profits. Crude oil was to be priced at the rates prevailing in the international market less a domestic market discount (usually 10–40 percent) to be agreed on with the investor. Stipulations regarding exploration schedules to be followed by the operator, the discount rate, and the Pakistani share in the equity of joint ventures to be set up following exploitable discoveries were to be negotiated case by case, depending on geological conditions and prospects.

Exploration increased as a result. During the fifth plan (1979–83), an average of sixteen wells was drilled each year—five exploratory and eleven for development. The private sector, including joint ventures with OGDC, accounted for an average of twelve wells—four exploratory and eight for development. A highly ambitious program of drilling, an average of fifty wells a year, is envisaged in the sixth plan. The record number of thirty-nine exploratory and development wells drilled in 1984 resulted in the discovery of four new fields.

An important development of considerable long-term significance is the discovery of oil in the Badin block south of Hyderabad. The first field to come on stream was Khaskeli in 1981, followed by Leghari in 1983 and Tajedi and Tando Alam in 1984. All were discovered by Union Texas except the last, discovered by OGDC. Occidental, another of the private oil companies participating in petroleum exploration and development, made a find at Dhurnal in the north in 1984.

With additional production from Khaskheli and Leghari in the south and from the Dhurnal field in the Potwar Basin, Pakistan's crude output in 1984 jumped to 19,700 barrels a day and has gone up further since to about 21,700 barrels a day—almost 25 percent of domestic oil requirements. This has not only brought to an end the downward trend that lasted from 1979 to 1981 but has also given rise to some optimism for the future, with production in 1984 already meeting 95 percent of the target set for 1988, the last year of the sixth plan.

The Occidental discovery at Dhurnal may confirm that the oil potential in northern Potwar is larger than previously thought and that oil can be found in economic quantities in geological formations older than those drilled so far. The Badin finds confirm oil deposits outside Potwar, which justifies the exploration program in the lower Indus Basin. But difficult drilling conditions in Potwar require the know-how brought in by private oil companies, and considerable seismic work and drilling are needed in the south, where OGDC holds the exploration license. Exploration could be accelerated if additional resources are mobilized through joint venture arrangements with oil companies acting as operators. Apart from Union Texas and Occidental, the three other companies currently assisting OGDC are majority-owned private Pakistan companies: Pakistan Petroleum Limited, Pakistan Oil Fields Limited, and Mari Gas Company (formerly Fauji Foundation).

OGDC's Challenging Task

OGDC, set up in 1961, is financed almost exclusively by the government through the annual development budget. This is because the large outlays it made were slow to yield corresponding increases in production. Moreover, pricing policies held down revenues. The price paid to OGDC for crude oil

Drilling operation at Toot oil and gas development project southwest of Islamabad. Toot project was aided by the first World Bank loan to OGDC for petroleum development.

produced at its largest field has now been raised from Rs44 per barrel ($3.50) to Rs201 ($16) per barrel, and similar increases have been agreed on for other oil and gas fields. As a result, OGDC's cash flow is expected to show a substantial improvement and permit it to finance 30 percent of its planned capital investments from 1985 to 1989.

Even with an improvement in its finances, OGDC's success will depend on whether it can recruit and retain qualified professional staff and operate as a commercial concern. To improve the availability of competent professionals, the government is embarking on a plan for human resources development for the energy sector. As a first step, it is undertaking an assessment of staff needs and the abilities of local institutions to meet those needs.

The government has identified a core investment program for OGDC which has three main elements: the appraisal and development of fields to be undertaken by OGDC using its internally generated funds and government allocations, exploration and development activities to be undertaken under existing joint ventures, and new joint ventures in prospective areas for which further efforts would be made by the government to mobilize private sector participation.

Although improved policies and performance will undoubtedly accelerate the development of domestic oil resources, the fact that proved reserves are modest should not be lost sight of. Estimated at 95 million barrels or 13 million tons, this will not last more than nineteen years at the 1984 rate of production. If probable reserves of 3 million tons and possible reserves of 6 million tons are added, the picture does not change significantly. Four promising offshore areas have been identified with the assistance of Norway, and arrangements have been made to undertake exploratory drilling. Since individual fields in the Indus Basin are small, new discoveries are unlikely to be large. This reinforces the need for developing natural gas, Pakistan's main fossil fuel.

Gas: The Tasks Ahead

The first gas discovery at Sui was made by Pakistan Petroleum Limited. A second find in Sind was made by Pak Stanvac (Esso Eastern) in 1957. Between them, they are estimated to have remaining recoverable reserves of about 9 million cubic feet, or three-fifths of the proven total for Pakistan. The two fields account for about 95 percent of current production. A large find was made at Pirkoh in Baluchistan in 1978 by OGDC. This is currently in production, along with two smaller ones at Sari and Hundi in Sind. Associated gas is being tapped from three Potwar Basin oil fields, but their contribution is marginal (less than 5 percent of the total).

Other discoveries have been made but have not so far been exploited because of the low calorific value of their gas. However, as a result of increased energy prices and continuing gas shortages, the development of these low-quality reserves has now become economical for power generation. The most important of these fields is at Uch, about fifty-five kilometers west of Sui. The calorific value of Uch gas is only about two-fifths of that obtained from Sui. In the context of shortages that are compelling Pakistan to shift to imported fuel oil for power generation, Pakistan must use this resource as fuel in power plants. Since the idea of upgrading the low-quality fuel for higher-value uses by eliminating its inert components is a doubtful economic proposition, the choice is clear-cut. The estimated recoverable reserves at Uch are 2.5 million cubic feet, equivalent to 18.4 million tons of oil. This is sufficient to meet ten years' consumption of petroleum products in Pakistan's power plants at the 1984 level.

A major effort is indeed under way to augment gas production and thus relieve the shortages that have plagued the country in recent years. Pakistan Petroleum Limited is embarking on a program to raise production from Sui's main reservoir by about 7 percent. Moreover, the output from the Mari field is expected to be raised by about 50 percent and from Pirkoh by 75 percent in the first instance and by about 200 percent at the next stage. OGDC also plans to develop the still untapped gas potential of the Dakhni field in northern Potwar. These developments will, when completed, increase gas output by about 30 percent to 1,200 million cubic feet per day. The target set for the last year of the sixth plan, 1988, will thus be met, enabling Pakistan to cope with average demand. However, shortages will persist during peak periods, and the shift from gas to alternative fuels for some key uses will have to continue. A vigorous exploration and development program could overcome such constraints because the probability of discovering additional gas reserves is high. More than a dozen prominent structures in the gas-prone areas are untested, and six one-well gas discoveries have not been fully evaluated. Existing arrangements for exploration and development under public and private auspices will have to be augmented to ensure better and quicker progress toward realizing the potential.

Private Participation

Given the limitations on what OGDC can accomplish, it will be necessary to draw in more private participation over and above what is envisaged in the sixth plan. This will require reoffering open areas—especially the promising ones—to companies willing to come in either on a joint venture basis or under service contracts. Expeditious development of gas fields such as Dhodak, Kothar, Nandram, and Uch will undoubtedly be facilitated if private companies are brought in to lend a hand.

The companies can now be expected to be more responsive to offers of leases. In the past, consumer prices were maintained at an artificially low level to encourage consumers to shift from imported oil to gas. This meant keeping producer prices equally low, a factor which inhibited private investment. The serious gas shortages of the early 1980s brought home the realization that this approach to pricing was counterproductive. The government has increased prices to consumers five times since January 1982 to raise the average to more than 54 percent of the border price for fuel oil, the nearest substitute. The objective is to move up to two-thirds parity by 1988, with progress now made easier by the fall in oil prices. There is thus increasing scope for adjusting producer prices upward for new discoveries. Under earlier arrangements in place since 1981, producers were allowed a discounted cash flow return of 12 percent by setting a base price indexed to the international price of fuel oil. This was not attractive to companies because the rate of return was too low in view of the exploration risks; the base price was set only after discovery, which raises the possibility of disagreements with the government on the interpretation of the cost-plus formula; and the formula itself was ambiguous with regard to the coverage of exploration costs.

Substantial changes have now been made because of the realization that the discovery and development of large additional gas reserves is the one event capable of making a dramatic impact on the fragile domestic energy balance. A bold step on producer pricing signals the government's determination to encourage vigorous exploration for gas. Under the new formula applicable since September 1985 for non-associated gas, the price paid to the producer for pipeline-quality gas will be 66 percent of the international price of fuel oil at main consumption centers adjusted for the transmission cost from fields to those centers. However, before exploration begins a percentage discount is to be negotiated that varies from area to area to take into account geological risk, anticipated costs, and market conditions. This discount will be a reasonable one to achieve the basic objective of accelerating exploration.

The World Bank's Role

The World Bank and its affiliates have been involved in the development of Pakistan's hydrocarbon resources for three decades, starting with loans for gas pipelines to link the Sui gas field with consumption centers. Relations with OGDC date from 1978 when funds were made available to increase oil production from the Toot field and to strengthen the capabilities of OGDC to enable it to play an increasingly effective role. A second loan for Toot was approved in December 1983 to raise its production further. Included in this loan was a component for continued development of OGDC's technical and managerial base, especially with regard to reservoir engineering. Another loan was made in October 1983 to revive gas exploration and to identify new oil and gas prospects in the hope of interesting private oil companies in participating in exploration and development. At the same time, a study was financed to help in mapping out a medium-term gas development plan. The Bank's support for a gas transmission and development project being executed by Sui Northern Gas Pipelines Limited has helped to mobilize export credits on very favorable terms, the first such outcome in a Bank-financed oil and gas project.

The Bank's lending has taken place in the context of changes in consumer and producer prices for gas, improvements in the technical and managerial performance of OGDC, and the creation of an environment for vigorous private participation in all phases of Pakistan's oil and gas industry.

In line with the progress made in these directions, the Bank made a $178 million loan in mid-1985 to support broad reforms in the energy sector and to assist in the implementation of a core program for augmenting energy supplies. This included a component for assisting the exploration and development of oil and gas fields, expanding gas transmission and distribution, and strengthening the infrastructure for the supply of petroleum products. Another loan was made simultaneously for OGDC to expedite the exploration and appraisal of resources in two areas assigned to ongoing and new joint ventures.

The energy sector loan provides a comprehensive long-term framework for policy actions and will serve as a basis for the Bank's expanded lending for specific energy investments in the next several years. The policy framework will also serve as a basis for more effective coordination of all external financing for the sector.

INDUSTRY
Maintaining the Momentum

PAKISTAN IS IN THE MIDST of an industrial revival. In marked contrast with the sluggishness witnessed during most of the 1970s, the rate of growth in recent years compares well with that of other countries in the region. The benefit to the economy from this revival underlines the importance of maintaining the momentum. With the government having decided to entrust primary responsibility for future expansion and diversification of industry to the private sector, its ability to fulfill this role is critically dependent on two factors.

The first factor is the policy environment. The changes since 1977 demonstrate that the dynamism of the private sector can be harnessed by policies which assure the safety of investment and the opportunity to earn adequate returns. Encouraged by the results, the government is now considering further policy reforms to consolidate the gains and build on them.

The second factor is the availability of both domestic and foreign resources on a scale commensurate with the needs of an economy in the midst of structural transformation. Pakistan faces a twofold task. It must find money to build new industrial capacity to cope with growing domestic needs and to tap the potential for exports in fields in which it has a comparative advantage. It must also make additional investments to modernize and upgrade existing industrial units to reduce costs and improve product quality. Although private investment has grown rapidly in volume in the most recent years—up by 22 percent in real terms in 1984—this may not be sustained unless the pool of national savings is enlarged. According to the latest available data, Pakistan's national savings amounted to only 11.2 percent of GDP, with the share of domestic savings a meager 5 percent.

The tasks ahead are formidable, but Pakistan's demonstrated capacity for overcoming challenges warrants confidence. Its industrial base has been built virtually from scratch because (barring a few textile mills) Pakistan had almost no large industrial units up to the time of independence in 1947. Even in 1960, the share of industry in GDP was less than 16 percent. Today, industry accounts for 23 percent of GDP and 19 percent of employment. Manufacturing now contributes 15 percent of GDP, with manufactured and semi-manufactured products accounting for 55 percent of exports.

Industrial Structure

Pakistan's largest industrial sectors are textiles and food processing. Each draws on inputs provided by a robust agricultural base. The two together account for more than half of value added in manufacturing. The other major sectors are engineering and chemicals. Intermediate goods such as cement, fertilizers, and steel have expanded rapidly in the past decade and are an increasingly important part of the industrial spectrum. A large labor pool, including some workers with industrially useful skills, an expanding supply of raw materials from agriculture, and the energy potentially available from river flows and gas are assets Pakistan can use to advantage to promote further industrial growth.

Manufacturing takes place in Pakistan in both the public and private sectors. The public sector is small in relation to the overall economy; in 1982–83 it accounted for less than 1.5 percent of GDP but accounted for 15 percent of value added in large-scale industry. Its strategic role in the economy derives from its substantial share in a number of principal industries—cement, fertilizers, chemicals, and heavy engineering. Within the private sector, in the 1970s the organized sector operating large and medium-scale units accounted for three-quarters of value added and 70–80 percent of total investment in manufacturing. The small-scale sector, which contributed the balance, is particularly important for the employment it provides. It also accounted for 30 percent of manufactured exports, major export items being carpets, sporting goods, cutlery, and surgical instruments.

The Industrial Policy Framework

Industrial policy in Pakistan has gone through three distinct phases. During the 1950s, Pakistan followed a policy of import substitution backed by high tariffs and import controls. During the 1960s, an export-promotion strategy was adopted without dismantling the structure of protection for domestic industry. In 1972, many agricultural processing units and large industrial establishments were taken over by a government concerned about the high concentration of industrial ownership. Ten industries, specified as of strategic importance for the future development of the country, were reserved for the federal public sector, and the existing units in these were taken under government control. This represented a far-reaching shift in policy for a country which gave primacy to private enterprise. Under the industrial policy enunciated within months of independence, only industries producing military hardware, hydroelectric power, railroad cars, and communications apparatuses were put off limits to the private sector. The government reserved, however, the right to step in to protect the public interest if there were inadequate private initiatives in these sectors. This intervention was to be a means of attracting private enterprise into such industries.

Since 1977, Pakistan has reverted to its initial policy. The industrial policy statement issued in June 1984 formalizes the shift. It reiterates the government's commitment to a mixed economy in which the private sector is to serve as the engine of growth and the public sector is to be only an investor of last resort, preferably in joint ventures with the private sector. The statement confirms the safeguards announced earlier against nationalization and limits public investment to the completion of ongoing projects and to the consolidation of existing units as necessary. The change in policy is reflected in projections of public and private investments in the industrial sector during the sixth five-year plan. The share of the public sector is set to go down from 56 percent in the previous plan period to 33 percent in the sixth.

In line with this change in economic philosophy, Pakistan is trying to improve its climate for private investment through changes in industrial incentives: it is easing barriers to entry by liberalizing the procedures to sanction new investments and private foreign borrowing. Recognizing the country's serious infrastructure constraints, its new industrial policy proposes to develop growth centers at which industrial facilities are to be concentrated. Industrial estates are to be set up in selected areas for this purpose, and the private sector is being invited to help establish them.

Barriers to Entry

Investment sanctions, the initial hurdle an entrepreneur has to overcome to make an industrial start, have now been eased because projects costing less than Rs300 million (with a foreign exchange component of up to Rs50 million) no longer require prior approval—except those on a long list of specified industries. The list includes industries of national importance, those for which programs have been set for enhancing indigenous content, and those covered by price controls or afflicted with overcapacity. Any foreign investment, irrespective of size, that requires more than 60 percent raw materials to be imported is also subject to prior approval.

While a further reduction in barriers to entry is indeed necessary, the procedural problems that arise in implementing a sanctioned project require parallel attention. In Pakistan's federal polity, many matters fall within the purview of provinces—among them the approval of the site of an industrial unit. Access to public utilities also falls within provincial control. This requires the investor to go through a time-consuming process of obtaining approvals from a number of authorities before work on a project can begin. A major constraint is the requirement that licenses have to be obtained even for imports freely allowed under the prevailing import policy. In instances where the same or similar items are included in the production plans of a Pakistani public enterprise, it is necessary to obtain a no-objection certificate from the latter—a requirement which often leads to further delays. Moreover, investors have to go through a separate exercise to obtain the support of financial institutions. The scope for coordinating approvals to reduce irksome delays has to be examined, both to accelerate industrial development and to attract foreign investors whose interest may otherwise shift to countries offering quicker and easier entry.

The structure of tariffs designed to provide incentives for domestic manufacturing is already under examination. A recently completed study showed some important anomalies, among them negative or inadequate protection for some industries in relation to value added at world prices but effective protection for many others. In about two-fifths of industries, tariffs are less important than quantitative restrictions (including import licensing and bans) and give protection in excess of that provided by duties. The government agrees that comprehensive rationalization of the system is needed and included preliminary measures in the 1985–86 budget as part of a long-term plan of reform for which an Incentive Reforms Cell has been created in the Ministry of Finance. Adjustments already initiated cover such industries as cement, iron and steel, chemicals, and pharmaceuticals.

Another area in which reform is under way is the policy governing prices set by the government for a number of important industries, among them cement, fertilizers, refinery products, and hydrogenated vegetable oil (vegetable ghee).

With a few exceptions, the government attempts to regulate returns within a range of 15–20 percent on assets employed for a given rate of capacity utilization. The arrangement provides insufficient incentives to minimize costs, allocate scarce capital efficiently, or promote optimal location decisions. Under its new industrial policy, the government is pledged to avoid the use of cost-plus pricing for new industries. Reliance on the market to set prices should be considered for existing enterprises as well as to ensure adequate incentives for reinvestment and improvements in efficiency.

Access to imported inputs has improved in recent years. This is reflected in a shift from a positive (permitted) to a negative (banned) import list and in the liberalization of imports of a large number of items. Despite this progress, tariffs remain high and the number of items subject to bans and other quantitative restrictions remains large. One consequence is uncertainty of supplies, which hampers production while the insulation from competitive imports reduces the incentive to efficiency in the domestic market. Unless Pakistani exporters have access to inputs at international prices, they cannot compete on equal terms in the world market.

Public Enterprises

Given the strategic role of public industrial enterprises, their efficiency has an important bearing on the economy's prospects. A principal constraint is the inadequate generation of internal resources, which was until recently a heavy burden on the budget. Current government policy requires public enterprises to finance all their investments through retained earnings and commercial borrowings. Of the several reasons why these enterprises can meet only a small part of their investment requirements from internal resources—only 14 percent in 1983—pricing policy is the most important. Out of their total sales, 90 percent takes place at administered cost-plus prices. The ex-factory price is in some cases uniform for a product throughout the industry; in other cases it differs from unit to unit to take account of varying costs. Since

Fertilizer being bagged at Lahore plant financed with assistance from International Finance Corporation, World Bank affiliate that assists private sector in developing countries.

profitability is thus determined for the enterprise from the outside, managers have little incentive to improve operational efficiency. There is also a lack of long-term corporate planning. To the extent this is done at all, it is by the holding corporation or the administrative ministry, the two upper tiers of management, rather than in the enterprise itself.

In a bid to move public enterprises toward a profit and

performance orientation, the government introduced in 1983 what is called a signaling system. It has three components: setting quantitative targets for each enterprise, monitoring performance to keep abreast of the results achieved by enterprises with reference to specified social and economic criteria, and bonuses to management for meeting or exceeding these goals. The system presently relies on performance indicators consisting of several components. The greatest weight is attached to enterprise profitability; volume of output, productivity, and energy consumption are also taken into account. Other relevant targets may have to be included to take account of social obligations imposed by government price controls and other external constraints.

Public enterprises continue to be governed by a multitude of regulations affecting the decisions of managements of individual units. The government has recognized that managerial autonomy is a main factor in improving the performance of enterprises. Many functions previously performed by administrative ministries have been delegated with this end in mind. But this delegation has not permeated downward in all cases. Some holding corporations have tended to retain too much detailed control over enterprises. Within the enterprise, delegation to individual managers to take the process to its logical conclusion has not been fully achieved.

A better managerial environment will not in itself remedy structural problems that make for poor efficiency. Some units suffer from a serious locational disadvantage because of decisions made in pursuit of the goal of greater regional equity. In others, technology has to be upgraded and the range of in-house production rationalized through more subcontracting. Plants which have run down through excessive use without adequate maintenance will need to be overhauled or replaced.

Financing for Industry

The financing of industrial development in Pakistan takes place primarily through the commercial banking system in conjunction with the development finance institutions. This is because the capital market is still not a significant source of funds for industrial investment. Although the government is trying to broaden the role of the market by setting up investment companies, introducing leasing, and promoting trading houses to market commercial paper, the role of the banking system will remain large for some time to come.

Commercial banks—particularly the five nationalized domestic ones—play a larger part in term lending for industry than in other developing countries. The sixth plan envisages that a third of private industrial investment will be financed in this manner. Such lending accounts for almost two-fifths of the banks' total advances. This is caused in large part by a policy that encourages these banks to provide the resources required by industry either directly or through consortium arrangements led by the development finance institutions. Pakistan has a number of such institutions set up to cater to different market segments. Notable changes in the industrial financing system during the last decade have been the creation of a number of nonbank financial institutions, the decline in the relative importance of established development finance institutions, and the emergence of the nationalized commercial banks as a major force in term lending.

The government's Islamization policy has changed the financial system since 1981. In place of the interest system, the concept of sharing profits and losses has been introduced; loans for working capital and long-term funds are provided based on participation term certificates in place of debentures. There are also companies which operate as investment funds on the same sharing basis in place of interest. Since terms and conditions between lenders and borrowers are not subject to restrictions that apply to interest-based banking, the effect has been to free the financial rate of return.

Foreign Investment

To augment the flow of funds to industry, the government wishes to mobilize foreign investment in the hope that it will bring technical and managerial know-how and market connections. Although the total capital owned by foreigners in the Pakistani corporate sector has increased—the rate of growth between 1974 and 1982 was 10 percent in terms of current rupees—the proportion of foreign capital to total capital has declined from 16.2 to 11.2 percent in the eight-year period. A significant part of recent investments came from nations that belong to the Organization of Petroleum Exporting Countries—at first from the United Arab Emirates and later from Kuwait and Saudi Arabia. This flow may be reduced as a result of the economic difficulties these countries are currently facing.

The current prospects for attracting increased aggregate flows do not look promising enough to meet the level of $150 million a year envisaged in the sixth plan. Although some industries offer good opportunities—oil and gas, fertilizer and chemicals, engineering and electronics—concern about safety of investment and of long-term returns seems to be holding back investors. This is another reason why the policy reforms on which Pakistan is now embarked have to be taken further to alleviate, if not eliminate, these concerns.

The World Bank's Role

The World Bank's strategy for assisting Pakistani industry has two complementary aspects: to strengthen and broaden the process of structural adjustment in the country's industrial sector and to support the government's efforts to revitalize the private sector through the provision of industrial finance. The industrial reform program is designed to improve the competitiveness of the sector in order to promote export expansion and import substitution. Issues being addressed include trade and industrial incentives, deregulation, the efficiency of public enterprises, pricing decontrol, and improvements in the credit delivery system.

The World Bank has participated in Pakistan's industrial development primarily by assisting development finance institutions in financing new industrial ventures. Three institutions have received loans. The bulk of the loans have gone to the Pakistan Industrial Credit and Investment Corporation to fund medium- and large-scale private projects. By 1982, eleven loans and credits totaling $274 million had been made to this institution. Three loans and credits totaling $80 million have been made to the Industrial Development Bank of Pakistan to directly make and refinance commercial bank loans for a large number of small industrial projects. Another $30 million has been made available to the National Development Finance Corporation to finance large public projects in manufacturing.

Since 1983, the World Bank's strategy for assisting Pakistani industry has focused on the system of industrial financing as a whole. The Bank's first industrial investment credit project expanded its assistance to Pakistan's financial system by using both development finance institutions and commercial banks as intermediaries for term lending to medium- and large-scale industries. Under this project, approved in 1983, the government rationalized regulations affecting development finance institutions in order to permit them to mobilize local resources and make working capital loans. These measures have increased competition among development finance institutions and provided more comprehensive financial packages to private investors. A second Bank industrial investment credit project, approved in January 1986, provides a line of credit to enable participating institutions to finance the foreign exchange requirements of investment projects of primarily private medium- and large-scale enterprises. The project will also broaden the Bank's assistance to commercial banks, the Karachi and Lahore stock exchanges, and participating development finance institutions.

Direct lending to industry has included assistance to three large fertilizer plants, a refinery engineering loan, and two credits for the small-scale sector—one for $30 million in 1981 and a second for $48 million in 1984.

In addition, the International Finance Corporation (IFC) has made investments in sixteen Pakistani enterprises totaling $182 million, of which about 6 percent was in the form of equity and the balance in loans. The IFC is also a shareholder in the Pakistan Industrial Credit and Investment Corporation and has thus contributed toward strengthening its role as a source of finance for the private sector. Among IFC-assisted enterprises, three are in the paper and pulp industry; two each are in textiles, food and food processing, and petrochemicals; and one each is in cement, fertilizers, steel, plastics, and word processing.

Also significant is the indirect contribution by the World Bank to industrial development through support for technical education and vocational training on one plane and for physical infrastructure on another. Work on the overall policy framework for industry has been advanced under the structural adjustment loan of 1981. This loan emphasized improving industrial incentives, increasing the efficiency of public enterprises, and streamlining investment licensing procedures.

HUMAN RESOURCES
Correcting the Lags

"THIRTY-FIVE YEARS after independence, Pakistan has a literacy rate below 25 percent and less than half the primary school going age children are in schools. These indices place Pakistan amongst the least developed nations, far below its rank according to other criteria, including the aggregate measure of per capita income. This status must be changed." This statement from the country's sixth five-year plan focuses on one serious handicap to its long-term economic and technological advance—its lags in developing human resources.

The handicap is, in a sense, historical: Pakistan started in 1947 with a primary school enrollment ratio of only 17 percent. Compared with that starting point, there has indeed been a substantial improvement in educational levels, with overall enrollment increasing by 5.8 percent a year during the 1960s and 1970s, and female enrollment by 7.6 percent a year. The inadequacies of today are a reflection partly of the low base at the start and partly of the low priority given until recently to education in development plans. With the population aged fourteen and under expected to increase by two-fifths from 1980 to 2000, the task ahead is challenging indeed.

Not surprisingly, spending on education has been lower than in comparable countries. Pakistan has never allocated more than 2 percent of GNP and 8 percent of public expenditures to the education sector; the comparable figures in other Asian countries are 3–6 and 12–15 percent. The problems posed by inadequate funding have been aggravated by wastage on one plane and a lopsided educational structure on another. The dropout rate in primary education is very high, with only 50 percent of those entering the first grade getting through the fifth. Wastage in higher education follows the same pattern of repetition and dropout.

Structural Anomalies

The structural anomalies in the system are evident from the wide gaps in educational attainment between urban and rural areas and between males and females. While almost three-quarters of urban children of the appropriate age cohort attended primary school in 1982–83, the proportion in rural areas was only two-fifths. There is the same disparity between sexes: nearly two-thirds of all boys were in school but only a third of the girls. In rural areas, the proportion of girls in school was only one in five. These differences are strikingly reflected in literacy figures: male literacy is 32 percent but that of females only 14 percent, with rural women averaging only 5.7 percent. The gaps in participation widen at higher levels of education. At the primary level, urban children are almost twice as likely to attend school as their rural counterparts, but by the high school level the disparity is 6.5 to 1.

If present trends continue, the number of illiterate citizens will grow from 45 million to 80 million by the year 2000. It is estimated that each year 4 million unschooled children and dropouts join the illiterate pool of those over five years of age. At the current rate at which adults are achieving literacy— 190,000 a year—it would take 215 years to deal with just the current number of unlettered people. Despite the endeavor made in recent years to step up progress, the actual outcome has been an unfortunate regression. As the sixth five-year plan notes, the participation rate at the primary school level declined from 54 percent in 1977–78 to 48 percent in 1982–

83, despite a rise of 24 percent in enrollments in the five lowest grades. In the same five-year period, the number of universities increased from ten to twenty, although the plan had provided for no additions. As the plan says: "nothing could portray the upside-down state of our educational system better than the coexistence of quantitative expansion of higher education and the falling participation rate of primary education."

The cost of educational backwardness is already high and will become higher still as labor inadequacies hold up Pakistan's quest for greater economic efficiency and productivity. For example, agricultural development has reached the stage at which new gains will depend on greater yields from the existing acreage because the chance of bringing additional land under the plow is nearly exhausted. Improvement in yields requires greater sophistication among farmers in the choice and use of inputs, making literacy and mathematical skills increasingly important. The fact that farmers in Pakistan are getting less out of high-yield crop varieties today than those in comparable areas of the region is attributable to poor husbandry caused in large part by poorer educational levels. High illiteracy among rural women places a heavy social and economic burden on them: they participate in a wide variety of agricultural activities in which more informed judgment could increase productivity. The role of women is even more important in relation to the health and nutrition of the family. Moreover, the lack of education among women has a strong negative effect on enrollment and attendance of children at the primary level, particularly of girls.

A poor educational base hinders progress in other sectors of the economy as well. Significant shortages exist at the craft level in industrial and construction skills—shortages aggravated by migration (mainly to the Middle East). At higher levels, the problem is less one of shortages than of quality and a mismatch between the skills acquired through formal education and the needs of the economy. In fact, the problem of quality is pervasive, as is brought out by the poor performance of many students at all levels of the educational pyramid.

The Need for Selectivity

The tasks facing Pakistan are very demanding, more so in the light of the constraints of resources. As the recurrent costs of education borne by the provinces continue to rise, it is becoming increasingly difficult to finance capital investments needed to expand facilities. Pakistan has thus no choice but to tackle the lags in education on a selective basis in line with a rational scheme of priorities. The country has wisely decided that broadening and strengthening its educational base has to take precedence; hence its renewed commitment to universal and compulsory primary education. The initial goal is a minimum five years of schooling, to be raised gradually to ten years. Upper primary and secondary education are also to be expanded but on a less ambitious scale, with the emphasis on catering to rural and female students. This is to be supplemented by a mass literacy program, relying largely on nonformal methods of education, which aims to impart literacy to 15 million persons in the ten-to-nineteen age group during the sixth plan period.

The sixth plan, like the one preceding it, envisages no further expansion of facilities for higher education of the general variety, urging attention instead to the improvement of quality to meet international standards. Particular attention is to be given to upgrading instruction in scientific subjects. To provide more equitable access, scholarships are to be given on a much larger scale than in the past to students from lower-income households to increase their participation in higher education.

Facilities for technical education are to be enlarged at the degree level and more so at the diploma and certificate levels. At the same time, arrangements for informal on-the-job training are to be expanded and systematized. There is an equal emphasis on improving the quality of existing institutions to make them more relevant to the needs of the economy. In a society which has to cope with increasingly complex technological challenges, it is indeed necessary to develop competence in specific branches of particular importance to the country. This explains the plan for centers of advanced studies and research in such fields as water-resource engineering.

Harnessing Private Resources

Recognizing that the twofold task of expansion and upgrading requires very large resources, the government recently decided to impose an education surcharge on imports to generate additional resources. Increasing use is also being made of funds collected through the *zakat*, an Islamic cess (tithe) on individual savings, to provide scholarships to poor students. But this is far from enough; the government is obliged to obtain a larger contribution toward costs from students, especially those receiving higher education. This is consistent with the objective of achieving greater equity in the educational system. The cost of educating a university student is substantially higher than that of educating a primary student. Since most of those at universities are from better-off families, and the returns from such education are high, this is reason enough to levy fees in line with costs.

The private sector plays at present a very limited role in providing education because of the nearly comprehensive nationalization of institutions in 1973 in support of a policy of free education. The additional burden this imposed on the government budget has been one reason for its inability to do more to expand facilities. The transfer of private institutions to public control also led to the loss of community support and interest, and often to a deterioration in quality. The private sector has now been allowed to open schools, and the government is committed to returning nationalized schools to original owners if this can be done without detriment to quality and coverage.

Another move to disperse and delegate responsibility for education is to give local authorities greater say in the planning, management, and maintenance of institutions providing basic education. One object is to get a larger local contribution toward costs, but the more important one is to promote community involvement—to motivate parents to send children to school and to generate local pressures for improvements in the relevance and quality of instruction.

Community Involvement

While Pakistan's broad strategy and priorities for education are appropriate, particularly its emphasis on primary education and improved access for rural and female students, the outcome may not match the ambitious goals that the country has set for itself because of the legacies of the past. The most important constraint is that the "felt" need for education is low among the poor, particularly in rural areas. The traditional reluctance to give girls an education is a factor to contend with, particularly in view of the policy to introduce mixed enrollment in all new and existing schools in the earliest grades and to provide separate facilities where this is not feasible.

A change in community and parental attitudes requires, as is now recognized, actions on two fronts. The first is to make the content of education less academic and more relevant to real life needs. The second is to improve the quality of instruction. Poor teaching and a lack of teaching materials contribute to poor student performance and strengthen the poor in their view that education has little to offer. Few rural children attending primary school acquire basic literacy and mathematical skills. Given the opportunity cost of sending children to school, this reinforces the disinclination to accept the sacrifice and perpetuates poor participation and high dropout rates.

The government recognizes that greater community participation is contingent both on increasing the number of schools to bring them nearer to the intended users and on improving quality. An imaginative step to utilize available community resources was taken during the fifth plan period

Student at government primary school for girls at Kala Gujran, Jhelum District, Punjab Province. School was built with World Bank assistance.

by starting schools in mosques, with a teacher provided to assist the imam in holding classes for children of both sexes in the three lowest grades. It is customary to send children to mosques to be instructed in religion. Linking this tradition with education in the three Rs makes it more acceptable because it is customary for children of both sexes to be brought together in mosques. The government is trying to reinforce local initiative by supporting mohalla (neighborhood) schools for girls, which have been started in many areas by women with some degree of educational competence. It is only through such cost-saving innovations that better progress can be made toward ambitious national targets despite resource constraints.

Nonformal and Secondary Education

Eradication of illiteracy among adults needs special attention in view of the backlog that Pakistan has to deal with. Since 1980 a central development and coordinating agency, the Literacy and Mass Education Commission, has been in charge of the effort being made through both government and voluntary agencies. It has done some good work in the area of functional literacy by developing instructional materials for such income-generating activities as the rearing of poultry. Many of these are being put on video cassettes, which rural people will be able to watch at village viewing centers that the government is setting up as part of its nonformal education network.

An open university, established with help from Britain and the USAID, expects to extend the range and quality of nonformal education by providing training materials for those engaged in literacy programs, whether on a salaried or voluntary basis. The federal government is backing these initiatives, but it will be necessary to develop supporting policies and institutions at the provincial level to underpin the work of the Literacy and Mass Education Commission and the open university. What both seek to do has to be done at the grass-roots level, which lies within the jurisdiction of the provinces.

With regard to secondary education, the government recognizes that it is the terminal stage for a majority of students. This implies that the curriculum should be flexible, emphasizing the development of job skills for the majority but offering also a strong academic orientation for the minority which will go on to higher studies. Another obstacle to both the expansion and improvement of secondary schools is the lack of adequately trained teachers. The shortage is the greatest in technical and science subjects, but in all disciplines it is difficult to find teachers willing to work in rural areas. Unless the agrotechnical courses have both the relevance and quality that enhance the employment potential of those taking them, the bias for the academic option among both educators and students may be hard to overcome.

The emphasis on improved teaching of science and mathematics at the secondary level is a necessary part of the endeavor to make education more relevant to the needs of the economy. The poor level of attainment at the secondary stage carries over into higher education and constitutes a particular handicap in engineering universities and colleges. The remedy in this case lies in upgrading the quality of teachers, teaching materials, and equipment. These are time-consuming tasks, which suggests that it would be better to adopt a gradual approach in implementing the program.

Higher Education

In higher education, the plan to consolidate rather than expand facilities may run into difficulties because of heavy pressure from a growing middle class for more student places. A composite solution would be to encourage more private higher education along the lines of the Aga Khan Medical Institute in Karachi. This will help to meet the aspiration of the educated middle class at levels of investment the government can afford, which should for equity include larger provisions for scholarships. More than a quarter of all educational expenditures is for higher education. It tends to receive more development funds than planned because of its higher absorptive capacity, thus aggravating the imbalance.

In technical education, quality is a serious problem. Notwithstanding migration to the Middle East, there are technicians who are unemployed because of inappropriate training. This underlines the need for linkages between employers and technical educational institutions at all levels (including polytechnics and monotechnics) to ensure that course content is relevant and market-oriented. The engineering universities and colleges remain largely undergraduate institutions. Limited progress has been made toward equipping them to offer more advanced programs, while facilities for research are practically nonexistent. This has to be remedied not only to meet the emerging needs of the economy but also to create a pool of better-qualified teachers.

Institutional programs for labor development will not by themselves be sufficient. At present, only 10 percent of the 50,000 skilled workers added annually are trained at public institutions. This points to the importance of private, nonformal programs to train employees on the job. The government can assist in making these programs more effective by evaluating and standardizing them through the National Training Board.

The World Bank's Role

The World Bank's involvement in Pakistan's educational program dates back to 1964, when an IDA credit was extended for the improvement of six polytechnics and the Lyallpur (later renamed Faisalabad) Agricultural University. Five further credits have followed with the dual objective of helping to meet the needs for skilled labor in agriculture and industry and broadening educational opportunities to provide better access to underprivileged groups. The IDA credits totaled $115 million as of June 30, 1985.

A credit was provided in 1970 to finance relocation and reconstruction of the Government Engineering College in Karachi. A credit in 1977 supported teacher training, agricultural extension training, and the expansion and qualitative improvement of the Sind Agricultural University. Another in 1979 was for improvements in primary education, especially for rural groups and females. The credit covered an experimental program to train teachers, build both houses for female teachers and classrooms, and increase supervision. The lessons learned from the experiment are to be incorporated into future programs. A credit given in 1981 was for vocational training to improve both the quality and output of institutions; to expand in-plant training programs; and to increase the government's ability to plan, manage, and evaluate skill training. A credit given in 1981, in continuation of the 1979 credit, is to improve the quality of primary education through better in-service training, closer supervision, and improvements in the supply of learning materials and physical facilities.

The World Bank's support in the coming years will continue to focus on increasing the literacy and basic skills of the population in line with Pakistan's own priorities. Further assistance will be provided for primary education to help realize the goal of making it universal. Help will also be provided for nonformal education to reach both children and adults who failed to get access to the formal system. Vocational training for the rural population and for women doing nontraditional work are two other directions in which the Bank expects to support Pakistan's efforts to improve equity in education.

OTHER TITLES OF INTEREST

On Pakistan

Gotsch, Carl, and Gilbert Brown. *Prices, Taxes, and Subsidies in Pakistan Agriculture, 1960–1976.* World Bank Staff Working Paper 387.

Jetha, Nizar, Shamshad Akhtar, and Govinda Rao. *Domestic Resource Mobilization in Pakistan.* World Bank Staff Working Paper 632.

Pakistan: Review of the Sixth Five-Year Plan. World Bank Country Study.

Squire, Lyn, I. M. D. Little, and Mete Durdag. *Application of Shadow Pricing to Country Economic Analysis with an Illustration from Pakistan.* World Bank Staff Working Paper 330.

On Other Countries

Korea and the World Bank
Yugoslavia and the World Bank

These publications are available from the Sales Unit, Publications Department, The World Bank, 1818 H Street, N.W., Washington, D.C. 20433, U.S.A. (Other World Bank publications are described in annual spring and fall catalogs and are listed in an index to the Bank's books in print; both the catalogs and index are available from the above address.)